Decorative Paper Craft

DECORATIVE PAPER CRAFT

Origami • Paper Cutting • Papier Mâché

First published 2016 by
Guild of Master Craftsman Publications Ltd
Castle Place, 166 High Street, Lewes,
East Sussex BN7 1XU

Projects first appeared in *Making Magazine*

Step photographs by the project designers; main photographs by Emma Noren,
Pete Jones and Laurel Guilfoyle; illustrations by Emma Cowley and Sarah Skeate.

ISBN 978 1 78494 174 1

PUBLISHER Jonathan Bailey
PRODUCTION MANAGER Jim Bulley
SENIOR PROJECT EDITOR Dominique Page
DESIGNER Ginny Zeal

Set in Berthold Akzidenz Grotesk
Colour origination by GMC Reprographics
Printed and bound in China

Contents

INTRODUCTION

Paper is undoubtedly one of the most affordable and versatile materials in a crafter's kit. A wonderfully adaptable material, paper is produced by pressing together the moist fibres of cellulose pulp derived from wood, rags or grasses, and drying them into flexible sheets. This is an ancient process, believed to have developed in China during the early 2nd century AD, although it may be even older than that – archaeologists have found fragments of paper dating from the 2nd century BC.

Paper crafts have long been a popular part of various folk art traditions, such as Chinese papercuts and Japanese origami. Thanks to modern manufacturing techniques, paper is now available in an extremely wide range of weights and colours, helping crafters bring these ancient traditions bang up to date.

If you want to create unique gifts for your family and friends, show-stopping party decorations and beautiful accessories for your home then look no further than this book. Simply grab some paper and get folding, cutting and sticking. Some of the projects can be drawn and cut out, while others will require more complicated techniques, but they all are fun to make and a joy to behold.

GIFTS

Money-box Bear

This twist on the traditional piggy bank makes a great gift for a thrifty friend. The shell is made from old boxes glued together, and the shape is built up with papier mâché then decorated. This box is deliberately designed to make it difficult to withdraw hard-saved pennies as it has no opening at the bottom — the owner has to wait for a rainy day to cut open the box!

You will need:

- Small cardboard box
- Scissors
- Cardboard tube and box from foil dispenser
- Egg box
- Thin card
- PVA glue
- Newspaper
- Bowl
- Paste brush
- Paints or tissue paper for decoration
- Varnish (optional)

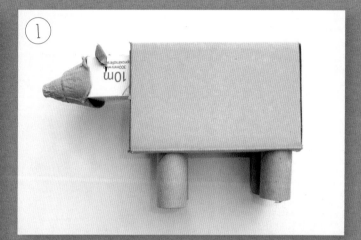

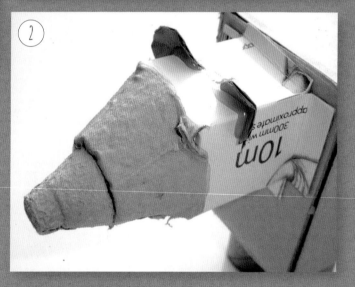

1 Choose a small cardboard box that will become the body of your money box. Carefully cut a slot in the top big enough to drop coins through. Cut the cardboard tube into four equal lengths to make the legs. The end of an old foil dispenser box and the cup of an egg box stuck together makes the head.

2 Use the indented bits of your egg box to make a snout and tail. Cut ears out of thin card and slot into the head. PVA glue can be used for sticking, but if you have a glue gun that also works well.

Tip
Make sure you prepare a good pile of newspaper before you start, as papier mâché can require a surprisingly large amount of paper!

3 Mix up a papier mâché paste using PVA glue and water. It needs to be about the consistency of custard. Rip the newspaper into strips about 3in (7cm) wide.

4 Before you start, it is important to entirely cover your cardboard bear with a layer of paste to allow the first layer of paper to stick properly. Begin by modelling the shape of your bear by taking fairly large strips of paper, covering them in paste and then scrunching them up into balls and sticking them onto the base. It is best to do this by getting really messy! Use your hands to cover the paper in paste and keep adding the scrunched-up paper until you have a shape that you are happy with. You will notice that if you add a lot of papier mâché to the head it will become heavy and unbalanced. If this happens, add more paper to the back end of the bear until it balances again. Be careful not to cover up the all-important coin slot in the top of your bear.

5 When you are happy with the shape of your bear, carefully paste over one or two flat layers of newspaper. Make sure that each strip is well pasted and smooth it down to work out any air bubbles.

6 Leave your bear to dry by a heater or in the airing cupboard overnight. When it is completely dry it will be very light but surprisingly solid. You can now paint and decorate your bear however you like. Pasting on tissue paper also works well. When complete, paste on a layer of PVA or varnish to protect and preserve your piece.

Pop-up Bunny Card

This pop-up card will happily stand out from the rest of the greetings on someone's mantelpiece. This project is a great introduction to the endlessly impressive techniques of paper engineering. Make your pop-up out of simple plain white card, brighten it up with coloured card or, if you're feeling even more creative, add some beautiful illustrations.

You will need:

- Templates on page 110
- Medium-weight card
- Pin
- Paper clip and ruler or bone folder
- Scissors
- Glue
- Scalpel and cutting mat
- Double-sided sticky tape

1 Photocopy or scan and print out the templates. Place the 'base page' printout onto a piece of card and, using a pin, prick through the paper to the corners of the page, the glue tab positions and the centrefold location.

2 Remove the template and score down the centrefold line, using a paper clip and ruler or a bone folder.

Tips

Don't rush… one wrong snip and you'll have to start again. Take it slowly at first and you'll get faster with time.

Instead of using a paper clip, replace it with a bone folder; it creases paper perfectly and is a great addition to a paper engineer's toolbox.

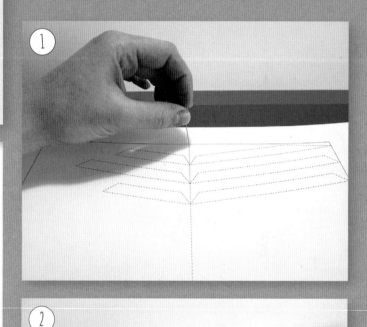

3 Cut the base page out using
your pricked dots as a guide.
Fold the base page in half,
down the pre-scored centrefold
line and place to one side. Take
the templates for the pop pieces
and stick them securely onto
your card.

4 Score the dashed fold lines on
the pop-up pieces and then on
a cutting mat carefully cut them
out using a scalpel.

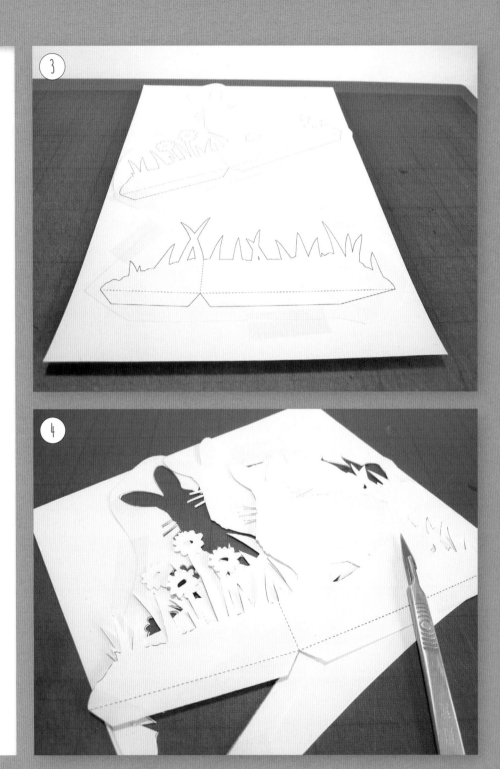

5 Stick thin strips of double-sided sticky tape onto all of the glue tabs. This is to be done on the front of the pop-up pieces, because the tabs will be folded backwards. Now fold all the pre-scored lines.

6 Using the pricked position guides on the base page, stick the pop-up pieces down onto the card.

7 Working front to back is the easiest way of doing this so as not to bend any of your creation.

8 Fold the card carefully to check the pop-up mechanism is working. Open again and hey presto – your pop-up bunny surprise is finished!

VALENTINE'S PAPERCUT

Send the one you love a romantic, personalized message with a delightful home-made Valentine's gift. Forget about store-bought presents and make your special someone this beautiful papercut so he or she will be in no doubt just how lovely you think they are. Take your time over this one because love can't be hurried!

YOU WILL NEED

- Template on page 114
- 15¾ x 15¾in (40 x 40cm) white card
- Tracing paper
- Pencil
- Lightbox or window (optional)
- Scalpel and cutting mat
- Eraser
- Spray mount (or other adhesive)
- 15¾ x 15¾in (40 x 40cm) coloured card/paper
- 15¾ x 15¾in (40 x 40cm) frame

1 Start by tracing the template onto white card; try to keep it fairly faint as any remaining lines will need to be rubbed out later. Depending on the thickness of your card, you may want to trace using a lightbox (or against a window if you don't have one). Once traced, begin to cut along the lines with your scalpel, holding it like a pencil to give you the most control.

2 It is best to cut out the design from the centre first, and may be easier to leave the cut sections in place until the whole middle section is finished, to give the cut-out some strength.

3 Finally, cut along the outside lines and carefully lift the cut pieces away, gently rubbing out any remaining pencil marks. Apply adhesive to the back and fix the cut-out onto your coloured card before placing in a frame.

Fans & Windmills

These paper fans and windmills make fun little gifts for children – and for grown-ups who want to relive childhood memories of long summer days spent on the beach. They only require small amounts of paper and are quick to make, so you can experiment with as many colours and pretty patterns as you want.

You will need:

- A few sheets of pretty paper, 12 x 12in (30 x 30cm)
- Scissors
- Glue
- Circular piece of card
- Stick/straw or string
- Template on page 111
- Pin
- 1¾₁₆in (2cm) circular card washer (you can easily make your own)

Paper fan

1 Cut 3–4 strips of pretty paper. The width of each strip needs to be the same.

2 Concertina fold each strip ⅝–1³⁄₁₆in (1.5–2cm) wide.

3 Glue the strips together into one long line, then stick the ends together to make a circle.

4 With the circle of paper standing up, use the concertina folds to push the top down into the centre. With a bit of gentle manoeuvering, this should create your fan shape.

5 Stick a circular piece of card into the back of your fan to hold all the folds in place.

6 Attach to a stick or hang it with some string.

Paper windmill

1 Stick two sheets of pretty paper together.

2 Photocopy and cut out the windmill template, not forgetting the holes.

3 Take a pin and feed it through the corner holes one by one (you may need a card washer on the pin before doing this if your holes are too big for the pin nib).

4 Feed the pin through the centre hole.

5 To finish, add a 1³⁄₁₆in (2cm) circular card washer and prick your pin through a stick.

BUTTERFLY MOBILE

Bring new life to old books by creating a beautiful sequence of light and airy paper butterflies. This pretty mobile will make a perfect gift for a stylish, vintage-loving friend, and it can be easily adapted with different illustrations and colours to match their tastes and the decor of their home.

YOU WILL NEED

- Various butterfly images
- Tracing paper
- Scissors
- Templates on page 114
- Pages from an old book, preferably with small text
- Beading wire
- Hot glue gun
- Wire cutters
- Hama bead mobile ring
- Natural jute string

1 Print out or photocopy your butterfly images onto plain paper and tracing paper; ideally you want at least one copy of each on both papers. Then carefully cut out all the butterflies, keeping the paper ones separate from the tracing paper ones. Put to one side.

2 Trace the butterfly templates onto sheets of vintage books (preferably sheets with small text) and cut out at least 30 butterflies and put to one side.

3 Cut a 20in (50cm) piece of beading wire. Lay one of the text butterflies down on the table and position the wire over the top so that the first butterfly is about 4in (10cm) from the end. Dab a bit of glue from the glue gun in the centre of the butterfly and place a colourful one on top.

4 Press to hold, then lift the wings a little.

5 Continue adding more butterflies to the wire, spacing them out and varying the colours, sizes and textures. You will need at least four butterflies on three wires, five butterflies on another three wires and three butterflies on four wires. Finally, make a longer wire with six butterflies for the centre of the mobile. Snip off any extra wire you have at the bottom with wire cutters.

TIPS

Using thin wire will make the butterflies appear to flutter in a magical way.

Why not cut organza butterflies and add those between the paper layers for a floatier look?

Don't stop at butterflies; add other insects!

6 Take the plastic Hama mobile ring and start wrapping the jute string around it so that the whole ring is completely covered except the holes, then stick the end of the string down with a dab of glue.

7 To hang the mobile, tie on three pieces of string each measuring about 11¾in (30cm) and tie to the ring at equal spaces then gather the ends and tie in a knot. To bring the mobile together start by hanging the mobile from a high point and tie the longest wire of butterflies to the knot where the strings meet in the middle, then gradually tie the rest of the wires through the holes of the ring in a random arrangement. Cut any stray wires. Finally, stick a few extra butterflies onto the actual ring with the glue gun and then fold open the wings on some of the butterflies to give a 3D effect. Gently blow on the mobile and watch your butterflies dance In the breeze!

Kusudama Flowers

It's hard to believe that simple brown wrapping paper can be transformed into a thing of such beauty. This is an easy paper craft project that makes a great, long-lasting alternative to the gift of a bunch of fresh flowers. They also look perfect as a table centrepiece when attached to wire stems or can be strung together to create a stunning paper garland.

YOU WILL NEED:

- 5 sheets of paper per flower – you can make any size, but here the paper was cut into 6in (15cm) squares
- Glue
- Florist's wire (optional)

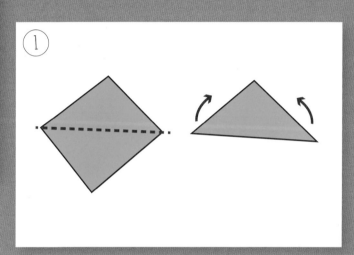

1 Lay a paper square down at a 45-degree angle, like a diamond. Fold the bottom corner up to the top, so that you have a triangle.

2 Fold the left and right corners of the triangle up to meet at the top middle, so that you have made a square.

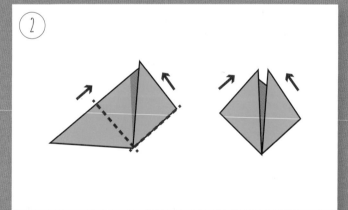

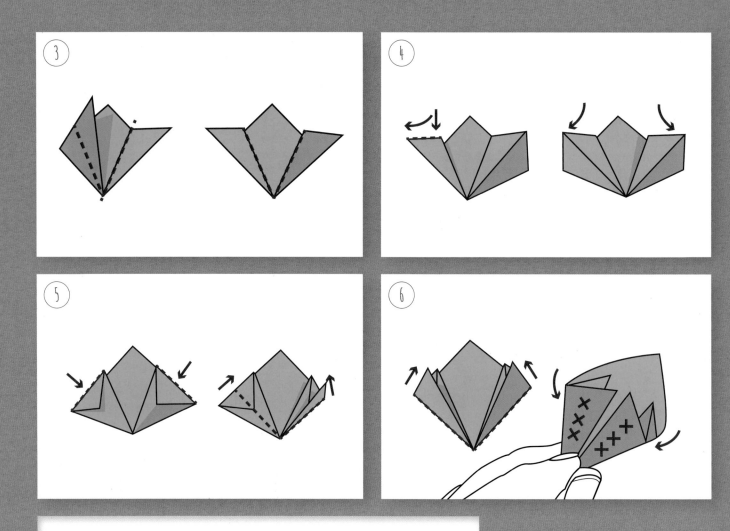

3 Fold the same points down.
The folded edge will line up
exactly on top of the outside
edge of the square.

4 Now open up the flaps that you
have just created, and flatten.
You are 'reversing' the fold along
the existing crease.

5 Fold over the top triangles so
that they are level with the edges
of the square behind. This creates
the three little petals on the inside
of your petal.

6 Fold the two long triangles back
on themselves, along the crease
you made earlier. Gently curve
and smooth the inside of the petal.

7 Glue the two facing triangles together to form the first petal. Hold firm until the glue sets. Repeat these steps to make five petals for each flower.

8 Now you have five petals, glue them together, along the edge of the join, one petal at a time. Make sure you wait for the glue to dry after every petal. Lastly, carefully insert florist's wire if you wish to attach them to stems.

MOROCCAN CARDS

Inspired by the geometric designs and bright colours that are characteristic of traditional Moroccan art and architecture, these striking papercut cards offer the perfect opportunity to experiment with bold graphics and contrasting colours. They could be sent as greetings or perhaps frame a set of cards to make a beautiful gift.

YOU WILL NEED
- Thick white card, at least 4¾ x 9½in (12 x 24cm)
- Scalpel and cutting mat
- Steel ruler
- Bone folder (optional)
- Templates on page 112
- Scissors
- Repositionable spray mount
- Coloured paper, at least 5⅛ x 5½in (13 x 14cm)

1 Cut out white card into rectangles 4¾ x 9½in (12 x 24cm) and use the handle of your scalpel or a bone folder, running along the edge of a ruler, to score down the centre so that when folded later your card will form a 4¾in (12cm) square.

2 Photocopy the templates and trim around each motif. Choose your first motif and give the back of the photocopy a light spray of glue and centre the template on one 4¾ x 4¾in (12 x 12cm) half of the card. Use only a very little glue, as you want to remove the template later on.

3 Using a sharp scalpel with care and working on a cutting mat, cut away the white areas through the template and the card below.

4 When your cutting is complete, carefully remove the remainder of the photocopied template.

5 Cut your coloured paper to 5⅛ x 5½in (13 x 14cm). With your card horizontally in front of you and the cut motif on the left, spray your coloured paper and stick it over the cut card, butting the right-hand side with the scored centreline, leaving an overhang along the three sides of about ⅜in (1cm).

6 Rub your paper firmly to ensure it's fully adhered to the card before turning it over and using the steel ruler and scalpel to cut the three sides flush. Fold in half to finish.

MEMORY BOOK

Take a sculptural approach to paper with this lovely twist on a traditional scrapbook. Containing plenty of pockets to store reminders of favourite holidays such as photos, stamps and tickets, a few simple folds will hold all the treasures in place. You don't have to stick to the travel theme; this would make a lovely gift to mark special occasions or landmark birthdays for loved ones.

YOU WILL NEED:

- 4 sheets of decorative paper (patterned on both sides), at least 10 x 10in (25 x 25cm)
- Compass or a plate to draw around
- Scissors
- Double-sided sticky tape
- Card (for the front and back covers)
- Patterned paper (to cover the book)
- Glue stick
- 10 large card tie-on tags
- Gum strip (optional) or sticky tape
- Ribbon
- Alphabet stamp set (optional)
- Photo corners (optional)

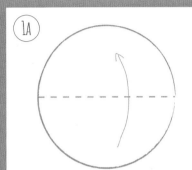

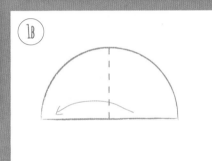

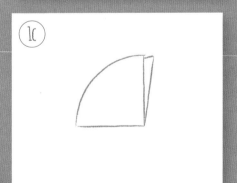

1 Using the double-sided decorative paper, measure and cut out four circles about 10in (25cm) in diameter. You can use a compass to measure this or use a plate as a template. The circles must be at least this size to make the finished book big enough to decorate and hold all your treasures. Fold the circle in half (1A) and then half again into quarters (1B & 1C).

TIP

Here an old atlas has been used for the patterned paper to tie in with the travel theme of the book, but you can choose anything you like.

2 Open out the circle and have the X-shaped folds facing you as shown in the picture, then fold the circle in half again from top to bottom. You should now have an X-shaped fold and a horizontal fold across the X. The X-shaped folds need to be valley folds (inverted folds) and the horizontal folds need to be mountain folds (the opposite to a valley), so re-fold at this point if you need to.

3 Bring the horizontal mountain folds towards each other so they meet in the middle (3A). You should now have a folded 90-degree segment of your book (3B). Repeat with the other three circles.

4 There are two inverted folds in each segment – one will be the 'floor' of your circle book when it is opened out and the other will be a pocket. To complete the pocket, you need to stick the open sides of the pocket together with a thin strip of double-sided sticky tape. Then, for decoration, fold down one of the top curved edges of this pocket. Repeat this on the other three folded segments.

5 Use one of the segments as a template for the cover. Draw around it on the card. Cut out the card and cover it with patterned paper. Repeat so you have a front and back cover.

6 Now glue all the segments together, making sure that all the 'floors' and pockets are the same way up. To make extra pockets from brown tie-on tags, fold the tags in half so that the straight edge comes to just below the hole on the other end. Stick the side edges together with gum strip if you have any, otherwise use sticky tape. Two of these pockets will fit on each 'wall' of your book, overlapping slightly.

7 Now glue the front and back covers on to your book, sandwiching the ribbon inbetween, in the centre of the curved outer edge of the book.

8 Now comes the really fun part of filling your book up with all your keepsakes and memories. Here, photo corners have been used to stick things down, and an alphabet stamp set to write titles and personalized messages.

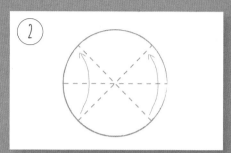

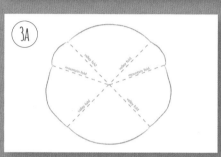

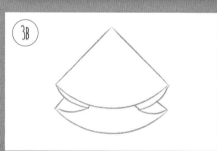

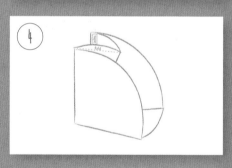

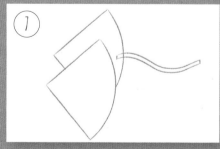

DIORAMA

A diorama makes a delightful, quirky gift and can be easily personalized to suit the recipient's tastes and personality. Made up of a box frame, rows of images are placed inside on strips, creating a three-dimensional scene. You can stick to a traditional scene or bring this antique art form up to date with some modern images.

YOU WILL NEED:

- 2 x A4 sheets of ⅛in (2mm) cardboard
- Scissors
- Decorative papers/images
- PVA glue
- Pencil/pen
- Scalpel and cutting mat
- Metal ruler
- Protractor
- Length of string

TIP

Play with scale by using smaller images in the back row and scale up towards the front.

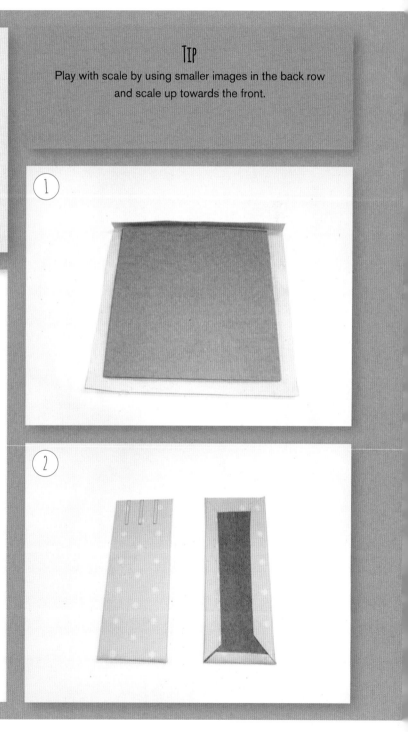

1 Cut out a 4⅓ x 4⅓in (11 x 11cm) square of cardboard and cover one side with decorative paper using PVA glue.

2 Cut out two rectangles 1⁹⁄₁₆ x 4⅓in (4 x 11cm) for the sides and cover each on both sides with the same decorative paper. These will form the sides of the diorama. Once the glue is dry, take one of the rectangular side pieces and, working from the centre (right side up), mark three points, ⅜in (1cm) apart. From each of the three points, mark another point approximately ⅛in (2mm) to the right. Draw a vertical line from the six marked points to 1³⁄₁₆in (2cm). Cap each duo of lines with a horizontal line. Now take the other side piece and place its short end against the drawn lines of the other short end and make a mirror copy of these lines. Using your scalpel and metal ruler, carefully cut out the slots on the cutting mat. Glue the two side pieces to the front outer edges of the papered square (from Step 1). The good sides should be facing inwards.

3 Cut out three strips of cardboard each measuring 4⅓ x 1³⁄₁₆in (11 x 2cm). Take one of these strips and glue it into the back slot (nearest the cardboard square). Cover this strip with papers and images of your choice.

4 Repeat this process with the middle and foreground strips to create your scene. Cut out another rectangle, this time measuring 4⅓ x 1⁹⁄₁₆in (11 x 4cm), and cover (as in Step 2). Glue to the top of the box opposite the slotted base.

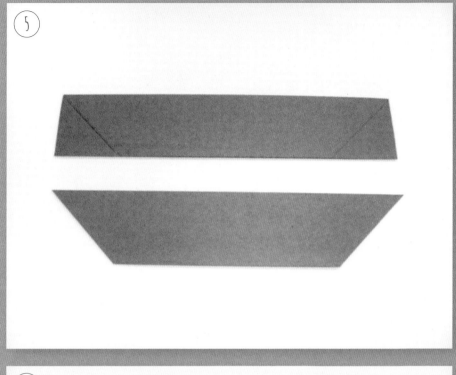

5

6

5 To make the diorama frame, cut out four rectangles of cardboard, each measuring 1³⁄₁₆ x 6in (3 x 10.5cm). Using a protractor, mark a 45-degree angle at each end and cut away the surplus card.

6 Cover each piece with decorative paper and leave to dry. Carefully dab glue onto the mitred ends and fix the pieces together to form a square frame. When the frame is dry, lay it onto the boxed scene to determine its final position. Drizzle glue onto the edges of the boxed scene and put the frame in place. Glue or tape a length of string to the back of the box so it can be hung on a wall if desired.

NOTELETS GIFT SET

A written note is a lovely, traditional way to say you're thinking of someone, and it is guaranteed to put a smile on the recipient's face. So why not make a pretty gift box and fill it with these floral notelets and matching envelopes? It will make the perfect present for friends and family alike.

YOU WILL NEED:

- Templates on page 118
- 8–10 sheets of thick white card (1 x A4 sheet per note card)
- 8–10 white 6 x 6in (15 x 15cm) square envelopes
- 10–12 sheets of plain printer paper (A4)
- Paper clip or bone folder
- Scalpel and cutting mat
- Ruler
- Glue stick
- A sheet of coloured thick card (1 x A3 sheets per box)
- Scissors
- Double-sided sticky tape (optional)
- Box measuring approx. 6 x 6in (15 x 15cm)
- Ribbon

1 Colour photocopy or scan and print out 8–10 note cards on thick card, 8–10 envelope liner templates on plain paper, 10–12 floral pattern sheets on plain paper, and one box template on plain paper. Score all the fold lines with a paperclip or bone folder on your note cards marked as a dashed line.

2 Carefully cut along the black solid line around the flower design then, using a ruler, cut between the crop marks shown in the corners. Fold all the note cards in half along the scored line and place them to one side.

3 Stick down an envelope liner template onto a floral pattern sheet then cut the template out. Repeat this process with the other templates and floral pattern sheets until you have the same amount of envelope liners as your note cards.

4 Take one of the envelope liners and slot it into an envelope.

5 Add a little glue onto the top of the liner and stick it down in place. Once dried, fold the envelope top down. Repeat this process with the other liners and envelopes.

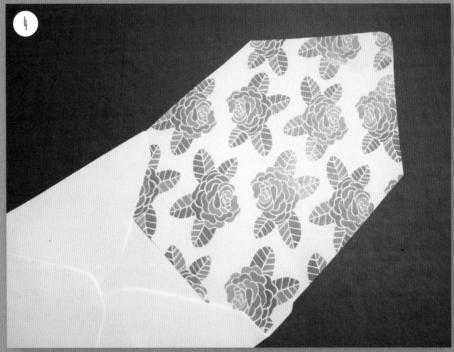

6 Score all the dashed lines with a paper clip or bone folder and then carefully cut the box out.

7 Using the letters on the template as a guide, add some glue or double-sided sticky tape to the tabs marked 'A' and 'D', fold inwards and stick down. Then put some glue or double-sided sticky tape onto the front side of the tabs marked 'B'. Fold and stick these tabs to the inner sides of the tabs marked 'C'. Finally, add some glue to the tab at the bottom (below the tab marked 'C') and fold it over and secure in place over the 'B' tabs.

8 Cut out a square of pretty floral pattern paper, around 6 x 6in (15 x 15cm) and stick it onto the inner base of your box. Place all the lined envelopes and folded note cards into the box. Fold over the box lid and tie a pretty ribbon around it. Your box and note cards are now ready to use!

TIP

Why not try to incorporate your own floral design to the note cards? Place your design onto a plain piece of card and carefully cut around it in the same way as the floral design shown in the templates section. You can then use the rest of the templates in the same way but with your own pattern.

Papercut Note Cards

A beautiful set of note cards is always a welcome gift. The technique of paper cutting is a great way to create traditional Scandinavian folk art designs such as these birds. This is a wonderfully adaptable project that you can make as simple or as complex as you wish. You can be sure that grateful recipients will be sending you thank-you notes!

You will need:
- Templates on page 111
- Tracing paper
- White or patterned paper
- Craft knife and cutting mat
- Scissors
- Craft glue
- A5 card to fold into A6 cards

Tips
To make interesting alternatives, use ink and a roller to give the paper some texture and colour.

Cut out multiples by layering the paper when you cut.

1 Trace the bird templates onto your paper.

2 Cut out the decoration inside the birds, first using a craft knife and then carefully cut around the outline using scissors. When cutting out with scissors, try to move the paper and not the scissors as you cut.

3 Using craft glue, stick your bird onto the folded card.

CELEBRATIONS

Floral Pom-Poms

Add real impact to your next party with these easy-to-make hanging pom-poms in a range of bright summer hues. Based on the shape of dahlias, these light tissue-paper creations will delight your guests as they float overhead. Have fun experimenting by making pom-poms in different sizes and colours.

You will need

- 8 sheets of tissue paper per flower
- Green wire
- Gold embroidery thread
- Scissors

1 Stack eight sheets of tissue paper together. Make accordion folds, creasing the paper carefully with each fold.

2 Fold a piece of green wire in half, and slip over the centre of the folded tissue; twist, trim and fold in the ends.

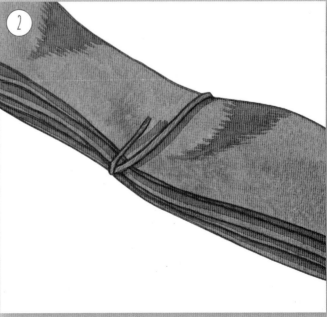

Tip

You can easily change the size of these pom-poms by increasing or reducing the length of your tissue paper.

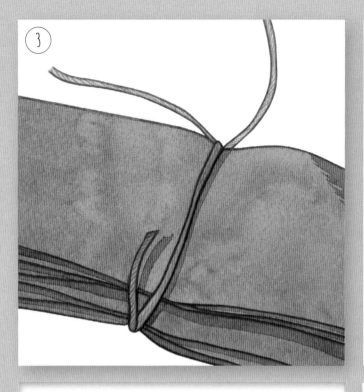

3 Cut a piece of embroidery thread and thread it through the wire then knot the ends.

4 Trim the ends of the tissue into rounded or pointed shapes with sharp scissors.

5 Separate the layers of tissue paper by pulling away from the centre one at a time until you have your desired flower shape.

BUTTERFLY CHANDELIER

A chandelier doesn't have to be made of crystal – paper and ribbon can look just as good! This summery chandelier will make a show-stopping centrepiece at a wedding party or other special occasion. The delicate butterfly cut-outs are easy to make with a punch, and a little bit of simple sewing ties the whole creation together.

YOU WILL NEED
- Butterfly punch
- A4 coloured card in 12 colours
- Sewing machine
- White sewing thread
- Flat florist's wire wreath
- Gingham ribbon

1 Start by punching out 20 butterflies from each sheet of card so you have 240 butterflies in total. Put to one side six sets of 12 coloured butterflies (these will be used later for the hanging butterflies on the chandelier).

2 Using a sewing machine on a tight tension, stitch the rest of the butterflies together, alternating them so that they face different ways.

3 Fold the butterflies in half so they don't lie flat.

4 Tie four lengths of ribbon around wire cross pieces.

5 Using the ends of the thread on the stitched butterflies, tie ends onto the inside circle of wire and loosely wrap the stitched butterflies around the wire so that the wire is no longer visible.

6 Take one of your six sets of 12 coloured butterflies and stitch them together randomly so some are from side to side and others are lengthways. Repeat with five other sets, so you are left with six strands of stitched butterflies. Take one strand of butterflies and tie one end to the first wire cross piece, tie the other end to the second wire cross piece (so the strand of butterflies are dangling).

7 Take the second strand of butterflies and tie one end to the second wire cross piece, tie the other end to the third wire cross piece and so forth until you have four strands of butterflies dangling around the outside of your wire.

8 Now take the fifth strand of stitched butterflies and tie one end to the first wire cross piece, tie the other end to the third wire cross piece.

9 Now take the sixth strand of stitched butterflies and tie one end to the second wire cross piece, tie the other end to the fourth wire cross piece, so you make a cross with the dangling butterflies across the middle of the wire.

10 Gather up the four ends of the gingham ribbon and tie in a bow together, so you can hang your butterfly chandelier up.

BLOSSOM BRANCH

Bring the spring inside with this paper blossom branch. Place some branches in a vase and use them to display Easter decorations or lay a single branch along your table to make an unusual centrepiece. And once you've got the hang of the technique, why not make more branches to celebrate the other seasons!

YOU WILL NEED

- Template on page 116
- 150gsm weight paper (thick paper/thin card) in similar tones of colour
- Bone folder or wooden skewer
- Scissors
- Hot glue gun
- Twigs

TIP

If your twigs are damp or 'green' allow them to dry out for a few days before attaching your paper blossoms.

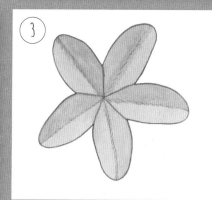

1 Use the template to cut out your blossoms in various complementary tones of paper. Use a bone folder or the end of a skewer (anything pointed but not too sharp) to score creases along the centre top of the petals to the centre of each blossom.

2 Now turn the blossom over and score another five lines from the join at the bottom of each petal to the centre of each blossom.

3 Fold the petals along the creases you have made to make them three-dimensional.

4 Use a hot glue gun to fix the blossoms to your twigs. Hot glue from a glue gun dries fairly quickly, so you just need to hold each blossom in position for a couple of seconds before it's firmly stuck. You could use regular glue, but this will take longer.

SNOWFLAKES

Turn your home into a winter wonderland with these intricate and decorative paper snowflakes. With some bright white card and a sharp scalpel, you can create these lovely Christmas decorations in either two or three dimensions and in a range of sizes. Leave them plain or add a little festive sparkle with some carefully applied glitter!

YOU WILL NEED:
- Templates on page 116
- Thick card (around 250–350gsm)
- Double-sided sticky tape
- Scalpel and cutting mat
- Glue and glitter (optional)
- String, ribbon or twine

1 Photocopy or scan and print out the snowflake templates – you can enlarge or shrink the templates to get different sizes.

2 Place the templates onto thick card and sticky tape them in place around the edges.

3 Using a scalpel and cutting mat, carefully cut your snowflakes out, not forgetting the string hole at the top. If you are creating a 3D version, it is a good idea to cut out the mechanism in the middle first.

4 Slot the snowflakes together if you are making a 3D version, or decorate your 2D version with sparkly glitter by sprinkling it over a light covering of glue.

5 Thread some string, ribbon or twine through the hole at the top and hang your snowflake up.

TIP
Always use a sharp scalpel blade,
as it will make the cutting out easier.

Christmas Crackers

Make your Christmas go with a home-made bang this year with these easy-to-make crackers. They'll look fabulous adorning your Christmas tree or as pretty table decorations for when friends and family come round. Choose coloured card and paper to match your festive home decor and have fun choosing the little gifts and writing the jokes to go inside!

You will need:
- Template on page 117
- Tracing paper and pencil
- Metallic card, 7½ x 14in (19 x 36cm)
- Scissors
- Rotary scorer
- Double-sided sticky tape
- Paper punch
- Wrapping paper cut into strips, 7½ x 14in (19 x 36cm)
- Cracker snaps, small gifts and jokes
- Silver string
- 2 sheets of pretty tissue paper

1 Photocopy or scan and print the template and cut it out. Trace the template onto the underside of the metallic card. Cut out the card and score along the edges with the rotary scorer as indicated on the template. Roll the card into a cylinder shape, folding along the scored lines to create a cracker shape. Stick the cracker together with double-sided tape.

2 Using a paper punch, punch a pattern along the short edges of the metallic card and along the end edges of the wrapping paper strips. Wrap the punched strip of wrapping paper around the cracker so that it is in the centre, and stick to the cracker base using double-sided tape.

3 Place a cracker snap, gift and joke in the centre of the cracker. Fold the cracker ends inwards and tie silver string around the smallest section to pinch together.

FOR THE HOME

Fairy-tale Papercut

Show off your paper-cutting skills by recreating a scene from this classic Brothers Grimm story, of the little girl with the red cloak and the big bad wolf. Both adults and children alike will be delighted by this charming picture, which would make a lovely addition to a nursery or a child's playroom.

You will need:

- Template on page 112
- A4 piece of good-quality paper or card
- Double-sided sticky tape
- Scalpel and cutting mat
- Very fine paintbrush
- Lightfast watercolour ink (red and black)
- 1 sheet of grey card cut to fit your box frame
- Paper clip (unfolded)
- Glue
- 8 x 8in (20 x 20cm) box frame

Tip

Try not to use thick paper or card, as your fingers will end up aching!

1 Photocopy or scan and print out the template – enlarge it if you would like a larger cutting.

2 Place it onto your paper or card and stick it in place with some sticky tape.

3 Starting from the centre, carefully cut away the grey area using a scalpel and cutting mat. Take extra care around the wolf and little girl.

4 Once you have cut and carefully removed the central area, start cutting the paper frame.

5 Your cutting is now ready to be painted. Using a very fine brush, add red ink to the little girl's cloak and black to the wolf. Leave to dry.

6 Now it is time to frame your cutting. Cut a grey (or another colour if you would prefer) piece of card to the correct size of the inner part of your frame. Using an unfolded paper clip, dab a little bit of glue onto the back corners and main structure of the cutting and place it in the centre of your grey card.

7 Add a little bit more glue in areas you feel may require it, such as the top branches of the trees, the wolf and the little girl.

8 Pop the cutting into the frame and admire!

HEARTFELT ROSES

Be warned — these paper flowers are so simple to make, they can become a little addictive!
Arrange them in any shape you like, experiment with colour and try out different papers.
You can use the flowers to decorate a parcel, make a wreath or use as a heart decoration
in a frame — there are so many possibilities to explore, so let your imagination run riot.

YOU WILL NEED
- Paper for the roses (paper from an old novel has been used here)
- Pencil (optional)
- Scissors
- Cocktail stick
- PVA glue
- Piece of mount board
- Picture frame
- Matte white paint (optional)

1 For each rose, take a piece of paper and draw a spiral on it. Cut it out with scissors. If confident enough, you could cut a spiral without drawing on the paper first.

2 Starting at the edge, wind the spiral tightly around a cocktail stick.

TIPS
For a romantic gift you could use the pages from your loved one's favourite novel: perfect for a first wedding anniversary.

If your scissors are sharp enough, you can cut three roses at a time; it speeds up the process, as you need quite a few roses for the artwork.

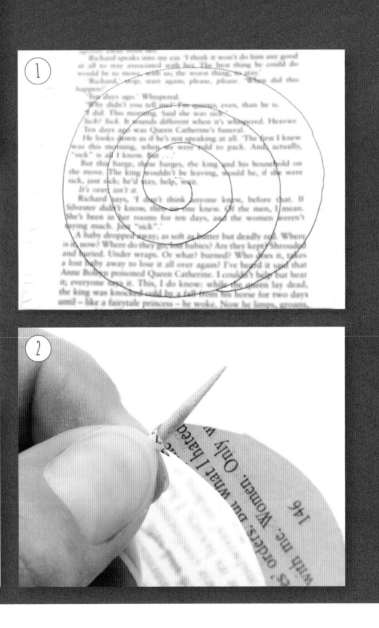

3 Take the spiral off the stick and wind it up almost to the end.

4 Place a good dollop of glue on the open end. Don't worry if the rose uncurls a little, it's meant to.

5 Now press the end against the spiralled rose.

6 Leave to dry completely.

7 For this artwork, place the roses in a heart shape and then one by one glue into place on the mount board. Find a beautiful frame and paint white (in matte if possible). Then hang on the wall and enjoy.

Woven Basket

This is an extremely therapeutic project and only requires cut paper and a little masking tape. It's an old traditional style of weaving that can be used to make decorative holders for cakes, sweets, fruit, plants or whatever you wish. Once you've mastered this technique we guarantee you'll be making baskets in all different colours and sizes!

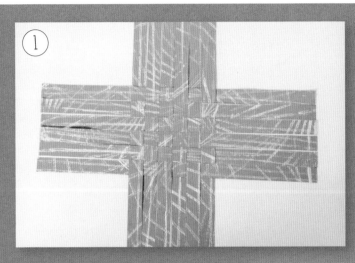

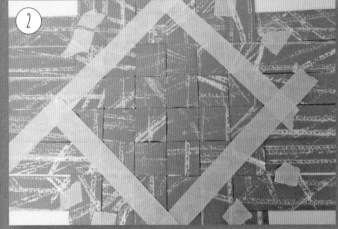

You will need

- Small piece of cardboard
- 1 x sheet of A2 cartridge paper (or 2 x sheets if alternating colours)
- 1 tube of paint (Daler-Rowney Pearlescent Tint was used here)
- A flat dish to put your paint in
- Scissors
- Masking tape
- Ruler

Tip

This technique can work with more strips but it's best to keep to six a side when learning.

1 Squeeze paint into the dish, then take your cardboard and dip the edge of it into the paint. Press it down onto the cartridge paper to make lots of striped patterns. Once you have covered the paper with painted stripes, cut 12 strips of paper (six of each colour if you are trying an alternating pattern) 1³⁄₁₆in (2.5cm) wide x 20in (51cm) long. Start weaving the strips together so you have six strips going horizontally and six strips going vertically. Keep the weave as tight as you can and the strips all equal distances from the main body of weaving.

2 When you have completed the weave you need to find the centre point along each edge of the tightly woven square. This will be in between the 3rd and 4th strip along each time. Take some masking tape and cut a piece approx 8in (20cm) long. Press it onto your clothes several times to take most of the stickiness away, then lightly press it onto your woven square diagonally from centre point to centre point. You'll end up with a diamond square shape. You can also add a few dots of tape along the tops of the strips so they don't all start unweaving for the next step.

3 Holding a ruler along one of the diagonal taped lines, fold the corner of the weave up and make a hard fold. Lay it back down and move the ruler to the next taped diagonal and repeat the folding process. Do this on all four sides so you have formed the base of your basket. Only score a fold on the woven area of the paper so you do not put any creases into the long lengths of strip.

4 Starting at one corner, unpick the long lengths of tape just at that corner and remove any smaller pieces you may have used attached to the long strips that will make that particular corner. Overlap the two strips at the very base of your basket and continue weaving them through the long ends. They will naturally follow the line of weaving. Add a dot of tape here and there to secure. Repeat this step, weaving the next two strips either side of that corner.

5   You will then need to move to the next corner and remove the length of tape, repeating the exact same process as in Step 4. Keep adding dots of tape but as you continue weaving, the basket gains strength and becomes easier to manipulate. You will have eventually removed all the long strips of tape and woven the corners into themselves, creating a closed basket with very long odd ends at the top.

6   Determine the height of your basket by starting with the shortest length of paper that's unwoven (let's call this strip 1). Bend strip 1 over its partner strip (strip 2). This is the strip that strip 1 crosses.

7 Slide strip 1 under one of the already woven strips and if it's long enough it may be woven a few times into the basket side. Make sure you cut the end of this strip so it doesn't hang out if it's too long.

8 Bend strip 2 back over strip 1 and weave the end of strip 2 into the basket. Keep repeating Steps 6, 7 and 8 to obtain a straight edge all the way round.

PATCHWORK PICTURE

Brighten up any room with a framed patchwork picture. This project is easy to create and can be made in any size or colour to complement your decor. All you need to get started is a selection of papers in pretty colours and patterns, and then have fun arranging the pieces. Why not make one for every room in the house?

YOU WILL NEED:

- A large square frame
- White/cream mount board or thick card
- Scissors, pencil and eraser
- 4 different pretty papers (2 x patterned, 2 x plain)
- Scalpel and cutting mat
- Spray mount or a glue stick

1 Measure the inside of your square frame. The best way to do this is to measure the glass carefully then cut out a piece of mount board or thick card to match the inner frame measurements.

2 Lightly pencil a square, 1in (2.5cm) in from the edge of your mount board or card, then note down the size of this inner square.

3 Divide this measurement by nine – this will give you the size you will need the patchwork paper pieces to be. Lightly pencil a 9 x 9 square grid (each little square measuring your patchwork paper size) onto the mount board or card.

4 On the back of each of your pretty papers, draw out 21 patchwork squares measuring the same as one of the squares on the grid. Then cut them out carefully, popping them to one side in matching pattern piles.

5 Erase the pencil lines around the edge of your inner gridded square on the mount board or card so you won't see any pencil marks once you have stuck the patchwork pieces down.

6 Number the paper piles 1 to 4 (preferably 1 and 3 should be patterned paper and 2 and 4 a plainer paper).

7 Lightly pencil numbers into each square on the mount board or card grid in the following formation:
1 – 2 – 3 – 4 – 1 – 4 – 3 – 2 – 1
2 – 3 – 4 – 1 – 2 – 1 – 4 – 3 – 2
3 – 4 – 1 – 2 – 3 – 2 – 1 – 4 – 3
4 – 1 – 2 – 3 – 4 – 3 – 2 – 1 – 4
1 – 2 – 3 – 4 – 1 – 4 – 3 – 2 – 1
4 – 1 – 2 – 3 – 4 – 3 – 2 – 1 – 4
3 – 4 – 1 – 2 – 3 – 2 – 1 – 4 – 3
2 – 3 – 4 – 1 – 2 – 1 – 4 – 3 – 2
1 – 2 – 3 – 4 – 1 – 4 – 3 – 2 – 1

8 Using the numbered grid as a positioning guide, stick down (with spray mount or a glue stick) your middle patchwork piece and then continue outwards evenly. Try to keep the paper pieces flush to each other to stop any gaps appearing.

9 Once all the patchwork paper is stuck down, pop the mount board or card back in the frame and admire your beautiful work.

Rolled Paper Bowl

If you have stacks of old magazines and catalogues that you no longer want but never get around to throwing out, this is the project for you. There are no expensive materials to buy, but lots of patience is required. Your efforts will be well worth it though, as your recycled paper bowls will add a cheerful splash of colour to any table!

You will need:

- 1 old catalogue or magazine
- Ruler
- Craft knife and cutting mat
- Fine knitting needle or crochet hook
- PVA glue
- Large bowl
- Plastic wrap

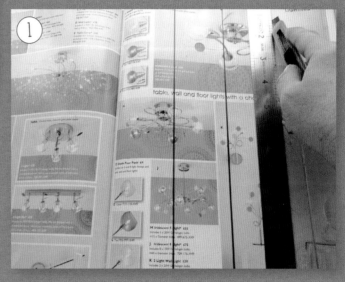

1 Using a ruler and craft knife, cut 2in (5cm) wide strips through as many pages of your catalogue or magazine as you can at one time.

2 Take one coloured magazine strip and lay it flat on the table. Using a crochet hook or fine knitting needle lay this on one corner of the strip so it is at a 45-degree angle to the corner. Then, much like rolling a piece of clay, use the same action and roll your knitting needle so it picks up the corner of the strip and rolls it into a long, thin tube.

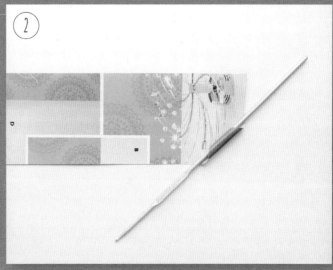

Tip

Vary the design by gluing several strips together to make much larger spirals, and cover some of the strips with kitchen foil to add a silver detail here and there.

3 Slide the needle out of the end and, using it lengthways, flatten the rolled tube of paper. Add glue all along one side of the flattened strip.

4 Take the same crochet hook or knitting needle and place it at one end and again roll the paper so it starts to spiral around the needle. After a few turns it is easier to slide the needle out and carry on spiralling the paper around itself with your fingers. When you get to the end, hold the completed spiral for a few seconds just so it can all adhere. Repeat Steps 2 and 3 so you make about 200 spirals.

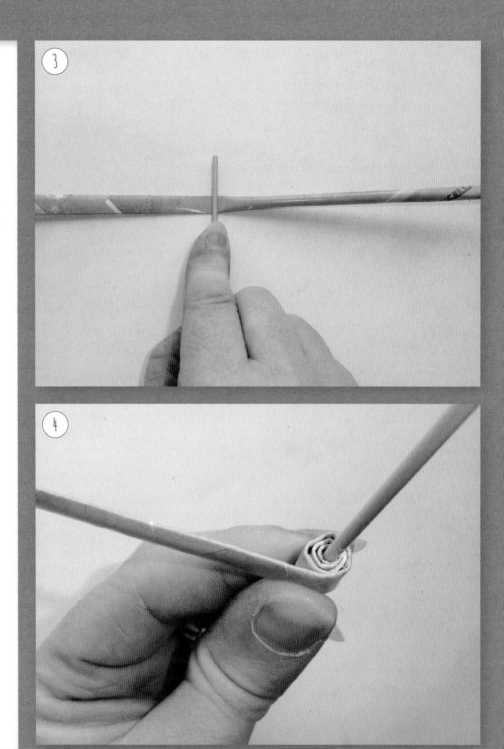

5 Take a large bowl and line it with plastic wrap. Then, working from the inside centre of the bowl, start placing in your spirals so they fit tightly together. Use lots of PVA glue on the edges of the spirals so they start to stick together. You will need to take your time here, holding the spirals tightly for a minute or two at each stage.

6 Leave the bowl in a warm room to dry completely. When dry, unwrap the plastic from the bowl. As you remove it, all the glued spirals should slide out of the bowl. The plastic wrap should easily peel away from the spirals, leaving you with the best coffee table bowl in town!

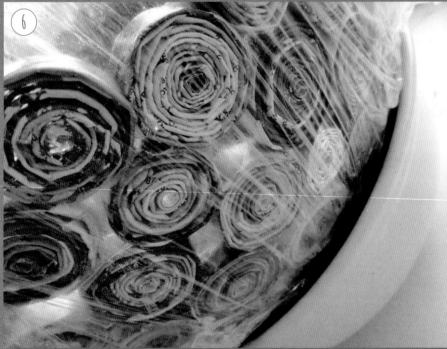

Cutaway Clock

Bring a bit of ornate beauty to every hour of the day with this striking papercut clock. This project is easier to make than you might at first think. You just need a little patience to work with the different materials, and the clock mechanism can be easily sourced from craft suppliers.

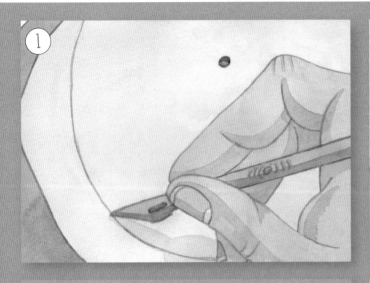

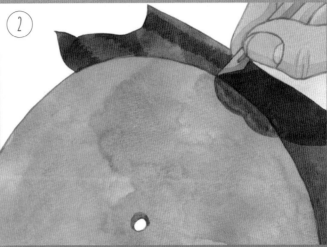

You will need

- Templates on page 113
- Scissors
- Sticky tape
- ⅛in (3mm) MDF board, 11¾ x 11¾in (30 x 30cm)
- Sharp scalpel, spare blades and cutting mat
- Drill (optional)
- Fine sandpaper
- Clock mechanism
- Wood-effect sticky-back plastic
- 11¾ x 11¾in (30 x 30cm) mount board
- Double-sided sticky tape
- Screw and screw driver
- Battery for the clock

1 Photocopy or scan and print out the templates then roughly cut them out. Sticky tape the back template around the edges onto the MDF board. Slowly and carefully cut the template out using a sharp scalpel. It's a good idea to cut the little hole out in the middle first – you can do this bit with a drill if it is fiddly. It can take a while to cut the MDF board, so try to be patient – it will be worth it! You may also need to change your scalpel blade regularly for both the MDF and mount board cutting.

2 Sand around the disk to make it nice and even, then check the middle hole fits your clock mechanism; this should be nice and snug – make the hole bigger if required. Stick the wood-effect sticky-back plastic onto the front of the MDF disk, making sure there are no air bubbles. Flip the disk over and cut all the excess plastic off, including the hole in the middle.

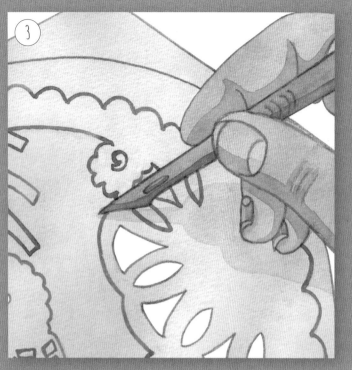

3 Stick the front clock template onto the front of the mount board and carefully cut out all the grey areas and outer line with the scalpel, starting from the centre and working your way outwards. Once it is all cut out, check the centre hole fits the clock mechanism with space around it, because if it fits too snugly it will stop the clock from working. Make the hole bigger if required.

4 Now add double-sided sticky tape to the back of the mount-board cutting, leaving the scalloped frame edge tape-free, as this doesn't need to be sticky.

5 Screw the clock back onto the clock mechanism then stick the clock front on top, making sure it is firmly stuck down centrally. Add the clock hands onto the mechanism, pop a battery in, hang the clock up and watch the time fly by!

FLORAL WALL-HANGING

This wonderful statement wall-hanging is decorated with beautiful handmade crepe-paper flowers. You can adapt the form, size and colours to suit your decor. This project explains how to make realistic-looking roses, peonies and carnations, providing enough inspiration to create a whole garden of paper flowers!

YOU WILL NEED

- Templates on page 115
- Craft scissors and serrated scissors
- Four different coloured packets of crepe paper
- Floristry wire and floristry tape
- MDF pre-cut letter
- Drill and ⅜in (1cm) drill bit
- Hot glue gun
- Wire cutters
- String
- Packet of floristry stamens

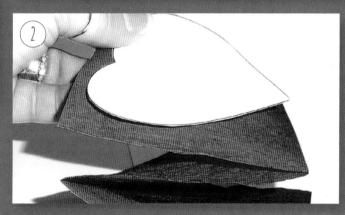

1 Photocopy all the templates and cut them out ready to trace onto the crepe paper. Cut strips of coloured crepe paper slightly wider than the templates you are going to use. You need to make sure the grain of the crepe paper runs vertically through the petals.

2 For all your template shapes, it is easiest to fold your crepe paper like a concertina, so you can cut several shapes at once. Make sure the petal or centre template fits before cutting.

TIPS

Using serrated scissors or pinking shears gives a very realistic effect for the carnations. You can also cut some leaf shapes with serrated scissors and add to your MDF letter to fill up any gaps seen from the front once all the flowers have been added.

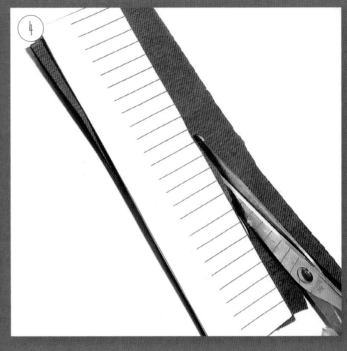

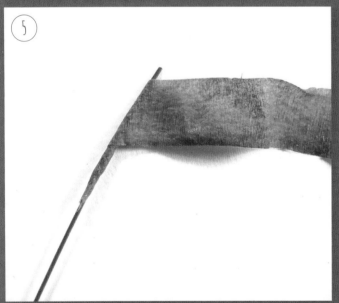

3 Holding your petal template securely, cut around it using craft scissors.

4 When cutting centres, also ensure the grain of the crepe paper runs vertically.

5 For all the flowers, wrap the very top of the floristry wire with floristry tape a couple of times. This will act as a grip for the first layer of petals. Make at least 30 flowers following the separate flower tutorials (see pages 94–7).

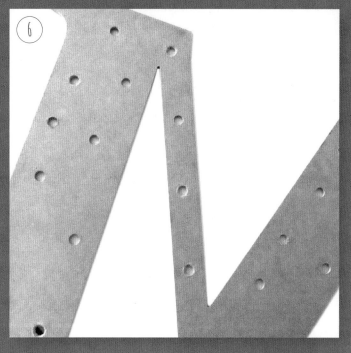

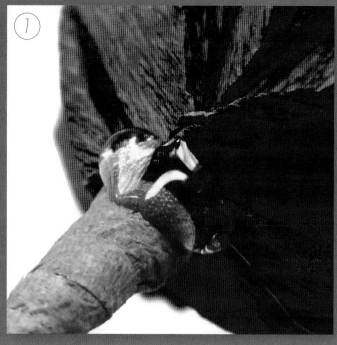

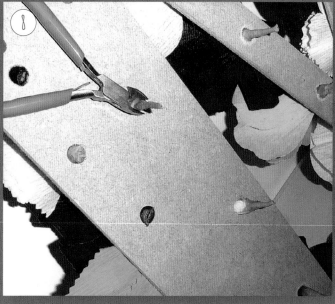

6 Once the flowers are made, drill ⅜in (1cm) diameter holes randomly all over your MDF letter. Do not drill them too close together, as this will weaken the shape.

7 Using a hot glue gun, add a dribble of glue to the underside of the flowers and push them through the holes on your letter until you have filled the shape.

8 Cut the stems short at the back using some wire cutters and tie some string to the top of the letter so that you can hang it up.

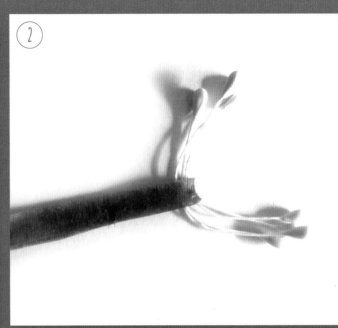

FLOWER TUTORIALS
Peony

1 Cut two fringed centres, six small petals and ten large petals. Roll one of the fringed centres around the floristry wire and secure in place with a small strip of floristry tape.

2 Take several stamens, cluster together and fold in half. Wrap a piece of floristry tape at this point to secure them all together in a bunch. Repeat this step to make four bunches per flower.

3 Hold your bunches of stamens along the stem of the wire so they are at the same height as the rolled fringe. Secure in place with floristry tape.

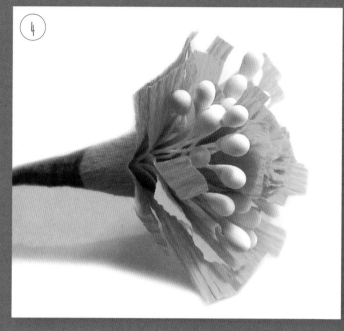

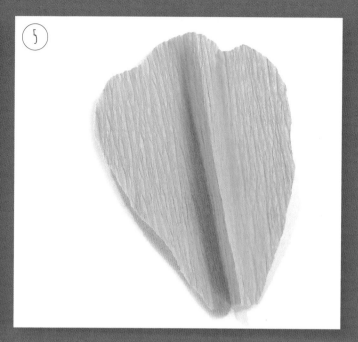

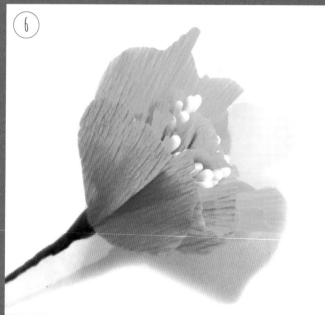

4   Roll the second cut fringe around the stamens and
    secure with more floristry tape.

5   Take a small petal and make a fold along the centre
    line. Secure this petal over the rolled fringe so the petal
    is positioned higher.

6   Add all six small petals one by one, securing each one
    with floristry tape as you go around. Keep repeating this
    step, adding the large petals in exactly the same way.

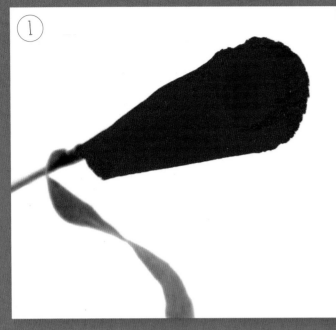

Rose

1 Cut six small petals and ten large petals. Take a small petal and roll your wire inside it so it forms a small cone. Secure it in place with a small piece of floristry tape.

2 Take another small petal and wrap it around the cone, again securing with floristry tape. Keep repeating this step, adding all the small petals.

3 Take a large petal and using exactly the same process as the small petals, keep adding one by one to create a full rose.

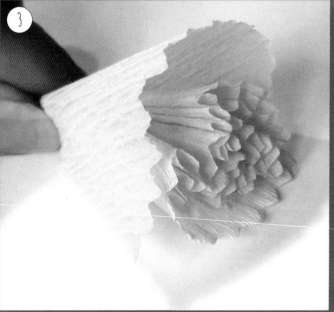

Carnation

1 Cut two serrated centres, six serrated small petals and six serrated large petals. Take one serrated centre and fold it like a fan, pleating all the way along. Secure it to the wire using floristry tape.

2 Take the other serrated centre and make another fan, again, securing it to the wire with floristry tape so they are tight together.

3 Wrap the small petals around the central fans one by one, securing each one with floristry tape as you go. Then, using the same technique, add all the large petals.

3D Flower Picture

If you're a fan of the minimal look, this picture will make the perfect addition to your home. This floral design is a beautiful way to add a little interest to your walls as a subtle hint of background colour is revealed by your carefully placed papercuts. You'll need to apply a delicate touch but the results will be stunning!

You will need

- Template on page 115
- Tracing paper
- Pencil
- 15¾ x 15¾in (40 x 40cm) white card
- Lightbox or window (optional)
- Scalpel and cutting mat
- Spray mount (or other adhesive)
- 15¾ x 15¾in (40 x 40cm) coloured card/paper
- Picture frame

1 Start by tracing the template onto white card – this side will be the back of your papercut and will not be seen when it's finished. Depending on the thickness of your card, you may want to trace using a lightbox (or against a window if you don't have a lightbox).

2 Once traced, begin to cut along the lines with the scalpel, holding it like a pencil to give you the most control. Make sure that you do not extend your cuts beyond the template lines, otherwise pieces may fall out.

3 When all the lines are cut, flip the card over. Gently pull the cut sections forward the desired amount from the petal tips. Apply adhesive to the back and fix the cut-out onto your coloured card before placing it in a frame.

Papier-Mâché Teacups

Keys, USB sticks, loose change and suchlike have a tendency to gather on surfaces around the home, making for a cluttered look. Worst of all, you can spend hours hunting for them, feeling sure you put them down just there... These fabulous papier-mâché teacups give you the opportunity to create vintage-inspired vessels in which to store all those bits and bobs!

You will need
- Plastic bottle (all measurements here are based on using a 1.5 litre bottle)
- Marker pen
- Scissors
- PVA glue
- Vaseline
- Newspaper
- Paintbrush
- Card
- Double-sided sticky tape
- Paper
- Paint

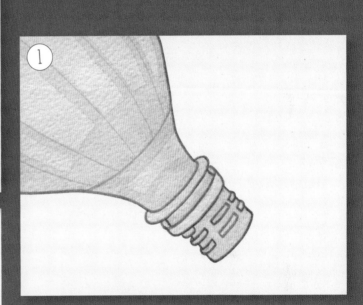

1. Take an empty plastic bottle and mark a line around the top section. Using scissors, cut away the bulk of the bottle, leaving a funnel shape to work with. Using the bottom section of the bottle as a container, mix two parts of the PVA glue to one part water.

2. Coat the inside of the funnel part of the bottle with Vaseline. Cut lots of strips out of a newspaper measuring approximately 1⁹⁄₁₆ x ⅝in (4 x 1.5cm). Coat your paintbrush with the PVA mix and pick up one piece of newspaper and place onto the greased inside of the bottle. Keep repeating this step so you completely cover the interior of the bottle with at least two layers of newspaper. Leave to dry overnight. Once fully dry, repeat this step so that you build up several more layers of newspaper. Again, leave to dry.

3 Fit your fist inside the bottle and twist the papier mâché shape around so it releases from the sides and slides out. Trim the top and bottom of your teacup shape using scissors so the edges are straight. Cut a small strip of card measuring ⅜ x 4¾in (1 x 12cm) and using double-sided tape, form a small ring with a diameter of approximately 1⅜in (3.5cm) and stick. Place this onto the bottom of your teacup shape and, taking more newspaper strips, build up more layers of papier mâché to hold it in place. Leave to dry.

4 Cut a circle of paper 3½in (9cm) in diameter and then draw an inner circle in the middle that is about 1⁹⁄₁₆in (4cm) in diameter. Using scissors, make inward cuts all around the edge of the paper circle, ensuring you do not cut past the drawn inner circle. Place this inside your papier mâché teacup so that it lies flat against the sides, painting on more glue to hold it all in place. Leave to dry.

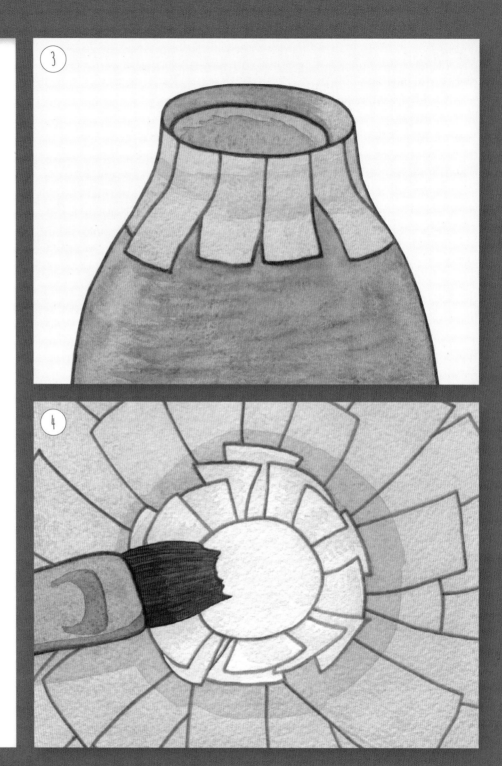

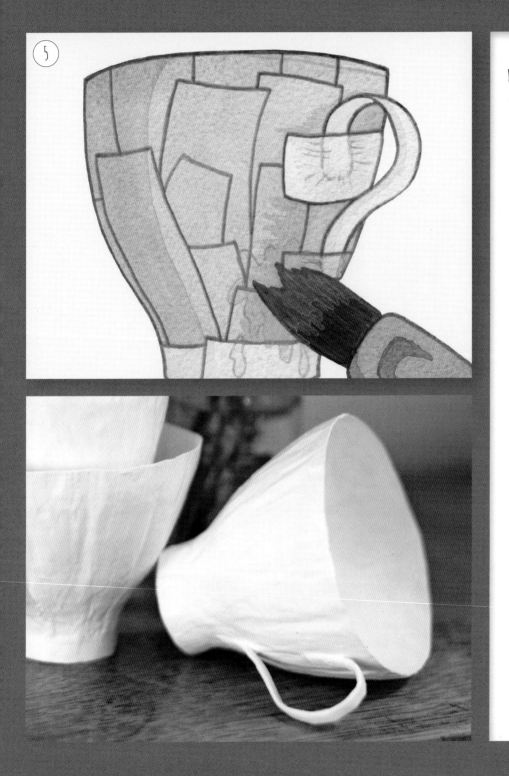

5 Cut a piece of paper measuring 4 x 2in (10 x 5cm) and roll it lengthways so you have a thin 4in (10cm) tube of paper. Slightly squash it and paint more glue onto it so it softens. Bend it into a handle shape and, using strips of newspaper, stick these at each end to hold it in place. Again leave to dry completely, then you can paint the entire teacup with any patterns and colours you like.

Book Sculpture

Decorating your home with interesting conversational pieces is all part of the fun when it comes to interior decorating. These striking, delicate book sculptures will certainly be a talking point. They are wonderfully easy to create, look beautiful and are simply made from old, unwanted books that you may already own or can find at your local thrift store.

You will need
- Templates on page 117
- A fat hardback book
- Scalpel and spare blades
- Glue stick
- Small cutting mat (A4)
- Pencil
- Ruler
- Double-sided sticky tape

Tip
Use your template as a cutting guide throughout the book; if you don't, your first and last page might not match up very well, which will make your sculpture wonky!

1 Carefully remove the hardback cover from your book with a scalpel – you want to keep the woven spine inside intact. Photocopy or scan and print out your chosen template. You may need to enlarge the template to fit your book height – to do this, measure the height of a page and scale the template to this size. Alternatively, you could design your own.

2 Cut around the template and place it onto the first page of your book, making the straight edge line up with the spine edge. Then carefully draw around it with a pencil.

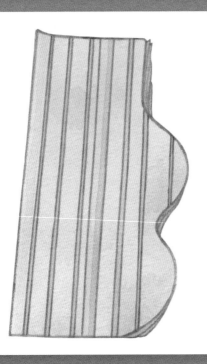

3 Slot a small cutting mat beneath the first few pages (around 5–8 pages) and then carefully cut along your drawn line. You want to be cutting through all the pages at once to get a clean cut. If this isn't happening, reduce the amount of pages you are cutting through. Remove the cutting mat and turn the cut pages over. Place your template on the next full page and repeat Steps 2 and 3. Continue doing these steps through the whole book. If your blade is ripping or catching the paper at all, it needs changing!

4 Once you have cut all the pages in your book, stick a few pages together at the front and back to strengthen – you'll need to do this for the next step. Cover the first page with double-sided sticky tape and then stick it carefully together with the last page, making sure the outer edge matches up. Fan out all the pages to make them evenly spaced apart, pop it in your desired location and admire.

Pretty Storage

Being organized around the home with box filing systems, storage baskets and bins is all very satisfying, but making them look pretty will bring you a whole new level of smugness and make all the difference to how on top of your clutter you feel! In just a few simple steps you can make your home office, children's playroom or living room look much more inviting.

You will need
- Decorative paper
- Scissors
- Glue
- Glue brush
- Double-sided sticky tape

1 Make a pattern for your boxes or bin by drawing up a template. Add ⅜in (1cm) all the way round for wrapping around edges. The bottom should always be a separate piece.

2 Cut out the paper – you may find it easier to do this in more than one piece so you are not dealing with large, unruly pieces of paper.

3 Apply glue to the item you are covering rather than the paper. Stipple or 'stab' the glue onto the surface using a flat-ended stiff glue brush.

4 Apply the glue to one flat surface at a time and smooth the paper out with a clean, dry, soft cloth. Stick the bottom on last.

5 Secure the last edge or end of the paper with double-sided sticky tape.

TEMPLATES

POP-UP BUNNY CARD

Photocopy at 200% for actual size

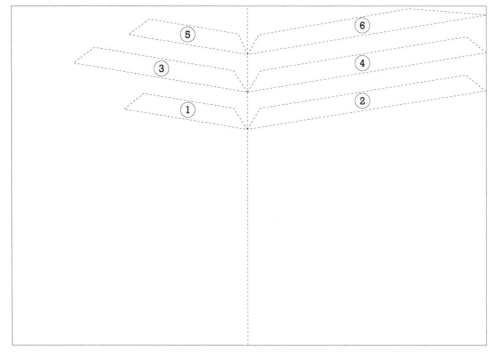

base page

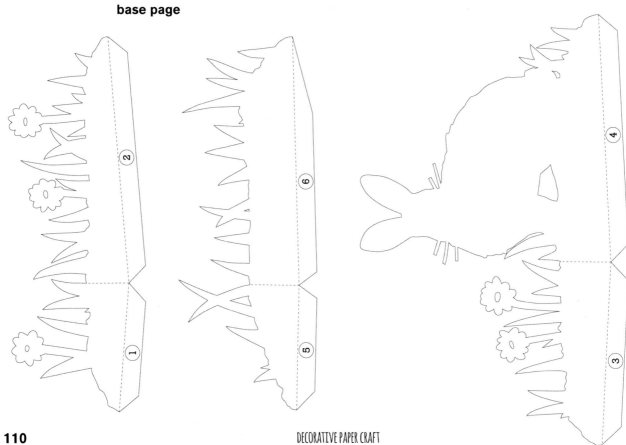

DECORATIVE PAPER CRAFT

PAPERCUT NOTE CARDS

Photocopy at 100% to make an A6 card

PAPER WINDMILL

Photocopy at 150%
for actual size

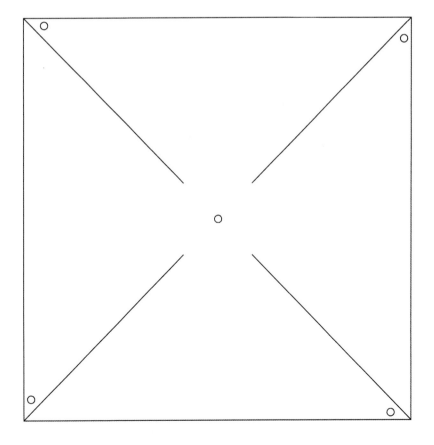

FAIRY-TALE PAPERCUT

Photocopy at
140% for A4 width

MOROCCAN CARDS

Photocopy at 200%
for actual size

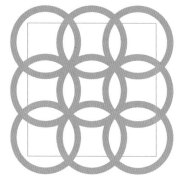

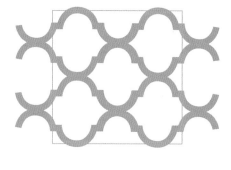

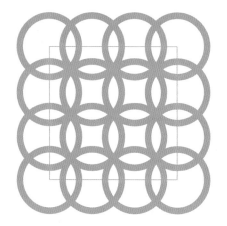

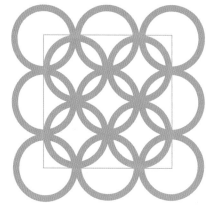

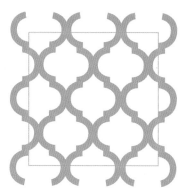

DECORATIVE PAPER CRAFT

CUTAWAY CLOCK

Photocopy at 200% for actual size

front

back

BUTTERFLY MOBILE
Photocopy at 125% for actual size

VALENTINE'S PAPERCUT
Photocopy at 320% for actual size

FLORAL WALL-HANGING

Photocopy at 200% for actual size

Carnation: centre

Carnation: petal

Peony: large petal

Peony: small petal

Peony: centre

Rose: large petal

Rose: small petal

3D FLOWER PICTURE

Photocopy at 250% for actual size

SNOWFLAKES

Enlarge or reduce to any size you'd like

BLOSSOM BRANCH

Photocopy at actual size

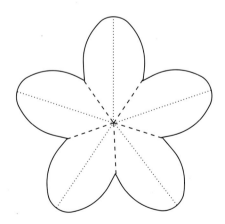

– – – Score on front

········· Score on back

DECORATIVE PAPER CRAFT

CHRISTMAS CRACKERS

Photocopy at 200% for actual size

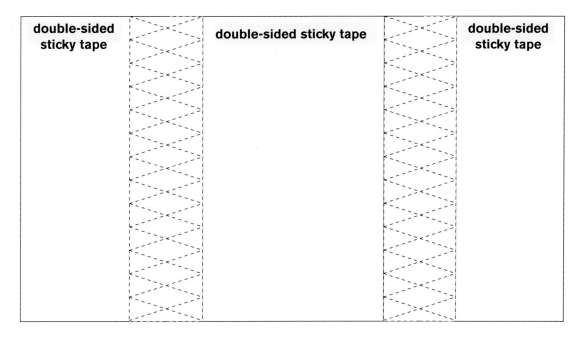

| double-sided sticky tape | double-sided sticky tape | double-sided sticky tape |

BOOK SCULPTURE

Photocopy at 160% for actual size

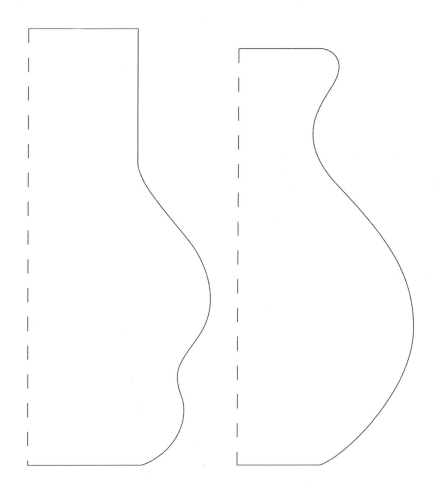

NOTELETS GIFT SET

Photocopy at 200% for actual size

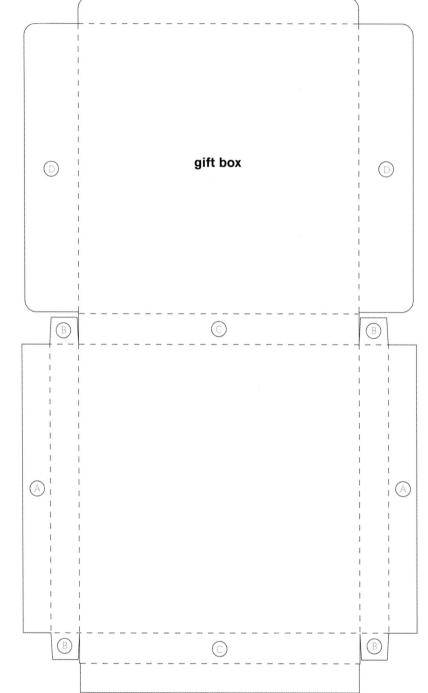

gift box

D

D

B

C

B

A

A

B

C

B

envelope liner

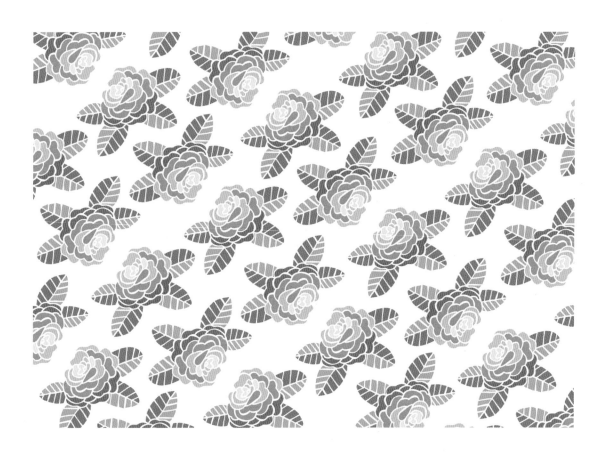

INDEX

To place an order, or to request a catalogue, contact:
GMC Publications Ltd
Castle Place, 166 High Street, Lewes, East Sussex, BN7 1XU
United Kingdom
Tel: +44 (0)1273 488005
www.gmcbooks.com